Praise for *Do No Work*

Too often the church simply dismisses the Sabbath as irrelevant. Andrew Gilmore boldly combats this misconception while skillfully applying God's Word in a modern context. *Do No Work* helps the believer honor God through the principle of ordained rest.

Pastor Daniel Sweet

Calvary Free Will Baptist of Norman, Oklahoma

In our 'time is money' culture, the tendency, at least for me, is to operate on the principle that rest is a luxury that must be earned. In *Do No Work,* Andrew Gilmore offers an alternate, biblical, and soul-satisfying point of view that made me stop and reconsider my beliefs about work and rest. If you think you're too busy to take a day off, read *Do No Work* and discover how the right kind of rest can bring peace into your life.

Erin K. Casey

Author of *Get Personal: The Importance of Sharing Your Faith Story*

As much as we like to keep moving in the hustle and bustle of daily life, we all need to rest. Not just take a break, but to intentionally rest. *Do No Work* is more than a book—it is a practical guide to a refreshed life.

Jim Woods

Writer at jimwoodswrites.com

Do No Work

Beat Burnout, Find Inner Peace, and Strengthen
Your Faith by Studying the Most Overlooked of
the Ten Commandments

ANDREW GILMORE

DO NO WORK: BEAT BURNOUT, FIND INNER PEACE,
AND STRENGTHEN YOUR FAITH BY STUDYING THE
MOST OVERLOOKED OF THE TEN COMMANDMENTS

PUBLISHED BY SEQUOYAH TRAILS PRESS

Cover Design: Liz Goodhead
Copy Editor: Amanda Price

This publication is not intended to diagnose or treat
psychological or physical ailments. While it is the opinion of
the author the advice offered is sound and biblical, you
should additionally seek the assistance of a qualified
professional for help therein.

Published in the United States by Sequoyah Trails Press

ISBN: 978-0-69229-608-0

To Jay Bratton and my mom who graciously gave me invaluable feedback.

To Katie who has supported me every (single) step of the way.

And to Jesus Christ, without whom, rest is impossible.

Contents

Part I
Beat Burnout

Part II
Find Inner Peace

Part III
Strengthen Your Faith

Do No Work

Beat Burnout, Find Inner Peace, and Strengthen Your Faith by Studying the Most Overlooked of the Ten Commandments

Why the Fourth Commandment?

A few years ago, for the first time in my life, I read through the entire Old Testament. As I did so, I was struck by how many times those books mention the Sabbath. God constantly reminded Israel of the importance of keeping the seventh day holy. Ezekiel says, "They utterly desecrated my Sabbaths" (Ezek. 20:13). Isaiah says, "Blessed is the one who ... keeps the Sabbath without desecrating it" (Isa. 56:2). Jeremiah says, "If you do not obey me to keep my Sabbath day holy ... then I will kindle an unquenchable fire in the gates of Jerusalem" (Jer. 17:27), and so on.

Even before God gave Moses the Ten Commandments, the Sabbath made an appearance. Shortly after the Exodus, God provided manna for the Israelites while they were in the desert. He told them to gather twice as much on the sixth day so they could rest on the seventh. And God Himself, after creating our universe, our solar system, our earth, and everything in it, rested on the seventh day.

This idea of a Sabbath rest runs deep in the DNA of the Holy Bible, yet as born-again Christians, we are wont to neglect it. We often sweep aside its significance, either because we don't understand it or because we don't really care. So I set out on a mission to try to understand the essence of the command to keep the Sabbath holy and to answer for myself a few questions:

- Is the fourth commandment still relevant?

- Why is something so prevalent in the Old Testament so overlooked by Christians?

- And most importantly, how should I behave on the Sabbath?

When I began my study, it was supposed to be short—a simple post for my fledgling blog. But the deeper I dug, the more I realized there is much more to the fourth commandment than I thought. In the process, I learned a lot about God, and I became a much stronger Christian as a result.

My hope is that this book will do the same for you.

The Case for the Fourth Commandment

A t Sinai, God gave Moses the Ten Commandments. This is number four:

Remember the Sabbath day by keeping it holy. Six days you shall labor and do all your work, but the seventh day is a sabbath to the LORD your God. On it you shall not do any work, neither you, nor your son or daughter, nor your male or female servant, nor your animals, nor any foreigner residing in your towns. For in six days the LORD made the heavens and the earth, the sea, and all that is in them, but he rested on the seventh day. Therefore the LORD blessed the Sabbath day and made it holy. (Ex. 20:8–11)

You may be asking yourself why you should devote your time to reading a book about the fourth commandment, especially considering that there are much larger issues at hand, such as murder, debt, infidelity, and bullying.

But when understood and applied appropriately, the fourth commandment addresses all of those ills. As a Christian, it is tempting to ignore or brush aside this commandment. To be sure, for the Christ follower, its significance differs drastically from its significance for Israel, for it is by the blood of Jesus Christ that we have our rest.

But why is it that we do not think twice about accepting the remaining nine of the Ten Commandments?

Commandments one through three address our relationship with God. Five through ten deal directly with our relationship with others. Commandment four, though, contains both elements, and it is the only commandment that speaks directly to how one treats oneself.

If you argue that the fourth commandment does not matter because it was intended for Israel, why would you not make the same argument for the other nine commandments? Essentially the matter boils down to two elements: morality and culture. It is easy to spot the morality in, "You shall not murder" (Ex. 20:13) but not so easy in, "Remember the Sabbath" (Ex. 20:8a). And the culture doesn't help. We simply do not value rest. Busyness is lauded, and idleness is of the Devil.

But when you become intentional about following the fourth commandment, and when you understand its deeper meanings, you will find it is more relevant than you once thought.

Part I

Beat Burnout

I will refresh the weary and satisfy the faint.
(Jeremiah 31:25)

CHAPTER 1

Two Ways to Beat Burnout (One Might Surprise You)

"**Y**ou're working this kid too hard. Look at him."

I hadn't even looked at myself. In fact, it had probably been a couple of days since I had looked in the mirror, except for maybe a passing glance. When I did, I realized what my cohort was talking about; I looked like hell. My eyes were bloodshot. My flesh was pale. My hair was too long and disheveled, and I hadn't shaved in days. Oh yeah, and my urine smelled like a Starbucks house roast.

But my boss wasn't working me too hard; she was working me a normal amount. *I* was working myself too hard.

Just before my last semester of college, a full-time job opened up where I had worked part time. I wasn't looking for full-time work; I just wanted to graduate. But after reading the job description, it seemed like a great fit for me, and I had this sense that God wanted me to apply. I can't explain it really, and it didn't make sense to me, but I applied anyway.

The interview came, and it was disastrous.

I was in Mexico studying Spanish when the team conducted interviews, so we did an interview over the phone. Now, I'm really old, so there was no Skype, and Google Hangouts was just a twinkling in the eye of Larry Page. So I used a good old-fashioned payphone. That's right. Remember those?

It was such a common thing to call the United States that there were hundreds of payphones scattered throughout Guadalajara, and they all had these special slots into which you could insert a phone card to dial internationally. This is all so primitive, right?

I got disconnected twice because I wasn't smart enough to figure out how to use those overpriced phone cards. And once I finally surmounted that obstacle, someone thought it would be a good idea to start his motorcycle right next to the phone bank, rendering communication impossible.

But I got the job. I guess God really did have a hand in it, because I know it wasn't my interview skills. I was ecstatic, but now I was committed to forty work hours and twelve hours of class time per week.

Most nights I was up until two or three or four a.m., only to be back at work by seven thirty a.m., which explains the Starbucks urine and bloodshot eyes.

What Is Burnout?

Burnout is not officially recognized as a disorder by the American Psychological Association in its *Diagnostic and Statistical Manual (DSM) of Mental Disorders*. But it is real nonetheless. No one questions the validity of stress and depression; often burnout is just their middle man.[i]

Because it is not recognized, there is no standard definition, but generally it looks like this: apathy and exhaustion brought on by distress, which can lead to feelings of inadequacy and clinical depression.[ii]

In the United States, an estimated 28.5 percent of workers experience burnout-related symptoms.[iii] With a problem so prevalent, would it surprise you to know that the fourth commandment has the recipe to prevent burnout? The issue is a complex one that worsened with the coming of the Industrial Age. Now in the Information Age we are always connected and always on call. But despite the pressure to be more productive and always available, there are two important things we can do to beat burnout.

1. Work

It may seem counterintuitive to work when work is often the cause of burnout. But work isn't actually the cause. The real cause of burnout is distress, and it just so happens that distress is usually brought on by work.

If you asked the random Christian what the fourth commandment is, he would likely say it is the commandment to rest. While that answer is technically true, it's like saying a checkerboard is black. Check out the second verse of the commandment: "Six days you shall labor and do all your work" (Ex. 20:9).

The fourth commandment, then, is also a commandment to work.

Now we might get down to semantics and say, "Well, the verse means that whatever work we have to do, we need to do it in those six days." Meaning if we didn't have any work to do, it would be okay to be idle. But there are at least two Scriptures that seem to indicate otherwise.

The first command recorded in the Bible is, "Be fruitful and increase in number" (Gen. 1:28). What does it mean to be fruitful? It means to be productive, to produce something of value. Both of these words *fruitful* and *productive* come from the agricultural terms *fruit* and *produce*. That makes sense considering Adam's original task was to take care of the garden in Eden (Gen. 2:5, 2:15). Of course this directive also refers to reproduction. But read verse 5 of the second chapter:

> Now no shrub had yet appeared on the
> earth and no plant had yet sprung up, for
> the LORD God had not sent rain on the
> earth and there was no one to work the
> ground.

There is a void implicit in this verse that God had man in mind to fill. This is even more overt in verse 15:

> The LORD God took the man and put him
> in the Garden of Eden to work it and take
> care of it.

So you see, God had in mind from the beginning for man to work. It is important to note that this directive came before the fall. As theologian Dr. Victor P. Hamilton puts it:

> Physical labor is not a consequence of sin.
> Work enters the picture before sin does, and
> if man had never sinned he still would be
> working. Eden certainly is not a paradise in
> which man passes his time in idyllic and
> uninterrupted bliss with absolutely no
> demands on his daily schedule.[iv]

Work is not a bad thing in the right context; God made us to produce fruit.

Second is this:

> The one who is unwilling to work shall not
> eat. (2 Thess. 3:10)

Work is good because without it, we cannot eat. What's more distressing than not knowing where your next morsel of food will come from? Yet even beyond physical needs, there is something distressing about not having work.

Why Work?

When I moved to Oklahoma in my senior year of high school, I went into a depression of sorts. My family packed up and left the dusty valley in northern Nevada known as Dayton to trek back to my parents' roots in the Midwest.

In Nevada, I worked a regular part-time job. In Oklahoma, I had no desire to work. Getting another job meant accepting reality. It meant accepting I lived in Oklahoma. But I thought of my situation as sort of an extended stay visit; I'd finish high school and then go to a university in some other city. I refused to let myself accept reality.

So instead I went into our spare bedroom that I affectionately called the "reading room," and there I would stay, spending hours upon hours reading novel after novel. The books helped me go somewhere I wanted to be—someplace I chose.

But I wasn't happy.

The irony is that, out of all the time I spent reading, I rarely did my schoolwork. And it was about a year until I finally got a job. My point isn't that a part-time job will make a teenager whole again but that God does call us to work, and He gives us meaning in that work. Subconsciously I understood going to work meant establishing roots.

Why did God want Adam to take care of the garden? He could have just dropped him off in Eden and said, "Enjoy!"

He knew Adam would feel unfulfilled. Just like Adam, we all want to feel like we do something that matters. God created us that way. As author and pastor Mark Buchanan writes, "There is sanctity in honest work. There is something in it that pleases, not just the eyes of man, but the heart of God."[v]

Society distorts our view of work because when supporting your family becomes your sole reason for working, of course you will feel disillusioned and empty inside. God gives us skills and passions and calls us to things much higher than just a paycheck. More often than not, money (whether too little or too much) just gets in the way. And let's not forget that the ultimate work is to do the will of God the Father (more on that in chapter 6).

Labor is good. It helps give meaning to our lives. It sustains us by bringing in fruit. And without meaning, we're all in trouble. In fact, loss of purpose is a central cause of burnout.[vi] This is (in part) why God said, "Six days you shall work."

Of course, work is just one variable in the equation.

2. Rest

This is what you thought I was going to say when you opened up the book, right? Well, I won't leave you hanging any longer:

> On [the seventh day] you shall not do any work. (Ex. 20:10)

This is what everyone thinks of when they think of the Sabbath commandment. And for good reason. The word *Sabbath* in Hebrew is *shabbâth*, derived from the verb *shâbath*, meaning to repose, to desist from exertion.[vii]

It may seem oversimplified, but rest is essential to avoiding burnout. Let's revisit agriculture for a minute. Consider corn. Any good farmer knows corn depletes the soil of nitrogen.[viii] If he plants only corn year after year, eventually the ground will cease to produce.

Sometimes the best way to be fruitful is to rest. This goes for people and for produce. God not only commanded Israel to rest every seventh day, but He also declared every seventh year to be a Sabbath for the land:

> For six years you are to sow your fields and harvest the crops, but during the seventh year let the land lie unplowed and unused. (Ex. 23:10–11)

God's reasoning is to let the poor eat what remains (v. 12), but there is also a very practical reason. Allowing the land to rest helps restore nutrients to the soil.

In the same way, we must cease work to avoid depletion. Work is necessary, but we were not made to work nonstop. We need to rest. I like the way author Dr. Joan Z. Borysenko states it: "The only workable strategy for maintaining productivity over the long haul is to learn how to relax."[ix]

We applaud busyness. Just go to a bookstore or library and count how many shelves are devoted to productivity. We all want to work harder, achieve more, and be more successful.

God knows this. He knew it before He formed us. Why do you think He rested after creating the universe? He didn't need to rest; God does not get tired (Isa. 40:28). Instead He ceased work on the seventh day to model the proper approach to labor. God knew if He did not command us to rest, we would literally work ourselves to death.

Now I doubt I need to go into the reasons why rest is good, so I will just give you this one thing: The National Sleep Foundation recently reported on driving while drowsy. You know what they found? Driving drowsy is just as bad as driving while drunk.[x] To quote the BBC: "In fact, 17 hours of sustained wakefulness leads to a decrease in performance equivalent to a blood alcohol level of 0.05% (two glasses of wine)."[xi] I'd venture to guess the majority of us regularly experience seventeen hours of sustained wakefulness. And impairment only increases the longer we stay awake. If that doesn't startle you, perhaps this will. The AAA Foundation for Traffic Safety determined in 2010 that nearly one in six fatal accidents involve drowsy drivers.[xii] And upwards of two hundred thousand automobile accidents per year are attributed to excessive sleepiness.[xiii]

So you see, you can be a complete teetotaler and still live like a drunk.

We need to make rest a priority in our lives.

The Prescription

The genius of the fourth commandment is that we have the prescription for the work/rest balance. Six parts labor to one part rest. What happens if you don't have work? You feel insecure, incomplete, unfulfilled (and probably hungry). What happens if you don't have rest? You become physically, emotionally, and spiritually exhausted.

The key here is balance. No matter how much we like our work, we must make time to rest from it. No matter how much we love rest, we have to work. This regular cycle of rest is God's mechanism for making sure we don't burn out.

Last, notice that the work comes first. We work the first six days and then rest on the seventh. Since time is circular, this may not seem to matter much, but the principle is evident: we are to take care of our work first. When we do that, it frees us up to rest.

Looking back, I cannot really tell you how I made it through that semester without failing a class or getting fired. But there is one thing I did. Every Sunday I made it a point to rest. No work. No schoolwork. Just church, food, football, and naps. Don't get me wrong, my faith wasn't all that strong at the time. In fact, I'd say it was kind of weak. But the effort I made to rest on Sunday without a doubt refreshed me.

Do these two things—work and rest—and you will be well on your way to beating burnout.

CHAPTER 2

How to Really Rest (for Real): Three Practical Ways

There's one thing about the fourth commandment you may find shocking. I know I did. The fourth commandment is about rest, right? But notice it never actually tells us to rest; it says not to do any work:

> Six days you shall labor and do all your work, but the seventh day is a sabbath to the LORD your God. On it you shall not do any work. (Ex. 20:9–10a)

I wrote in chapter 1 that "Sabbath" comes from a verb meaning "to repose." This is true, but it only tells half of the story. A more literal translation of the verb *shâbath* is "to cease, to abstain, to desist from."[xiv] So you see, God did not command rest; He commanded Israel to desist from work. The commandment does make use of the word *rest* but only when referring to how God "rested on the seventh day" (Ex. 20:11). In Hebrew this word is *nûwach*, a more straightforward word for rest.[xv]

Let me be clear: we should rest. There are (at least) three verses that explicitly command rest on the Sabbath: Exodus 31:15, 34:21, and 35:2. Nevertheless, the wording of the commandment is important. Why did God use *shâbath* instead of *nûwach*? By using the word *sabbath*, God tells us not just that we must rest but *how* we should rest. He draws a clear distinction between work and repose, making it explicit that Israel should not labor on the seventh day.

Using that as a foundation, here are three ways to rest (for real).

1. Get Physical Rest

We all know about this kind of rest. Rest from shoveling dirt, from moving furniture, from chasing the kids. This is probably what most of us think of when we hear the word *rest*. In physics, work is when "an object is moved through some displacement while a force is applied to it."[xvi] In English, work involves movement.

For centuries this has been the obvious definition of work. Farmers plowed fields, carpenters built buildings, and servants drew water from the well. This was certainly true in the context of the fourth commandment too. Israel had just escaped a life of brick making under the whip of Pharaoh (Ex. 1:11).

Industrialization has complicated our understanding of work, replacing much of the labor once done by humans with technology. But using this basic definition is an important place to start because at its core, work means sweating, lifting, grunting, pushing, and pulling. And it doesn't take a physicist to know what the opposite of movement is.

Psalm 46:10 tells us, "Be still and know that I am God." That's good advice for those who wish to rest. And if you're interested in beating burnout, physical rest is an essential component. Neglecting sleep (and other needs) is one of burnout's primary stages.[xvii]

So put off yard work for another day. Wait until tomorrow to vacuum. Be still.

2. Get Financial Rest

Had God said, "You shall rest" (*nûwach*) instead of, "You shall not do any work" (*shâbath*), we could interpret the command to mean that we should rest from physical work only. I could do all of my labor the first six days, and then "rest" on the seventh by working on profit and loss statements at my abacus. Since I'm not physically laboring, I'm following the commandment, right?

But rest is not just ceasing from physical labor; to truly rest, we must also rest financially. In fact, the more I study the fourth commandment, the more I am convinced it is about money. Read verse 10:

> You shall not do any work, neither you, nor your son or daughter, nor your male or female servant, nor your animals, nor any foreigner residing in your towns.

It is interesting that God specifies all of these parties. The commandment says our animals and servants should rest too. If the commandment were meant just for Israel, then why is this there? Animals cannot sin. They are programmed to obey.

And none of the other commandments have this list of people who need to follow it. Nothing like, "Thou shalt not murder. Neither you nor your servants nor your animals shall murder." Why not?

It comes down to money.

Wealthy landowners (once Israel entered the Promised Land) could rest on the Sabbath but still require their servants and animals to work. In this way, they would obey the commandment but still make money at the same time. But God didn't want that. He wanted Israel as a whole to rest. As Matthew Henry writes:

> All works of luxury, vanity, or self-indulgence in any form, are forbidden. Trading, paying wages, settling accounts, writing letters of business, worldly studies . . . are not keeping this day holy to the Lord.[xviii]

God wants us—for one day—to take our minds off of money and focus on eternal things. He knows in this world we have to manage our assets, protect our losses, work, and provide food for our families.

In the twenty-first century, this is no big revelation. For us work and money are synonymous. It's the only reason why many work at all. So asking us to give up moneymaking activities one day out of the week could be thought of as a tithe of our time, a tithe of our attention. God is a realist. He knows the limitations of our flesh demand us to focus on survival. Therefore He asks only for one day of rest.

The Levitical tithe is one tenth of our income (27:30). But consider this. There are 168 hours in a week. One tenth of that number is 16.8 hours. That number is roughly the amount of time an adult is awake on any given day.

At first glance it may seem like we are losing out on a big chunk of cash—about 17%—by ceasing work every seventh day. In fact, resting actually increases our productivity because it allows for refreshment of the body and mind. It is when one works consistently over a period of time without rest that he gets burned out.

And remember Malachi 3:10?

> Bring the whole tithe into the storehouse, that there may be food in my house. Test me in this," says the LORD Almighty, "and see if I will not throw open the floodgates of heaven and pour out so much blessing that there will not be room enough to store it."

The same applies for time. Give God your time, and He will honor it if your intentions are pure. He will bless you with productivity like you've never seen before. We all value time, so by giving some up, we honor God.

But let's get one thing clear. Just like with money, God does not need your time. This commandment is for our benefit (Mark 2:27). God set up this Sabbath boundary so we would have a healthy view of time and money.

3. Mental Rest

But maybe you have these two things down. You don't earn money on the Sabbath, and you don't do any heavy lifting either. There is a third way we must rest or else risk burning out. We must rest mentally.

As a teenager, I was always in church on Sunday—at least physically. Living in the Pacific Time Zone meant that NFL football games began at 10:00 a.m., right around the same time the worship service began. So I'd sit in my seat, sing the songs, and hear the sermon. But my mind was often with the Kansas City Chiefs.

Physically I was at church, but mentally I was elsewhere.

Though our bodies are at rest, our minds may be working. We make mental lists of things we need to take care of when we get in to work on Monday. We stress out over that exam paper due on Thursday. But we cannot truly rest if our minds are focused on work.

The book of Amos has some words to speak to this idea:

> Hear this, you who trample the needy and do away with the poor of the land, saying, "When will the New Moon be over that we may sell grain, and the Sabbath be ended that we may market wheat?" (Amos 8:4–5a)

These people were not working on the Sabbath. They weren't selling anything, but they were counting the minutes until they could. Their minds and hearts were still in business mode. In this way, they broke the fourth commandment without physically doing a thing. Professor James L. Mays says it better than I can:

> What matters this keeping of holy days, this proper piety in the sight of God and man, if all the while they are straining toward the 'unholy days' when their true dedications to greed fills the time? Once again the prophet shows the failure of faith which accompanies the success of religion, for the business they were so eager to continue was the enterprise of betraying their Lord.[xix]

Rest from work is a literal and physical thing; we need to physically rest from work. But we also need to turn our mental focus away from work.

But we can't just not think; what should we do with our minds? That's what I need to talk to you about...

CHAPTER 3

Want Better Rest? Don't Forget This One Word

Try to think about nothing for thirty seconds. Absolutely nothing. Go.

Chances are that instead of thinking about nothing, you were thinking about thinking about nothing. Or about meatloaf. Or about that ugly brown car you saw on the side of the road. Or about the full moon you saw last night.

When meditating, why are you supposed to focus on breathing? It is because we are made to focus on something. Dwelling on a repetitive activity as basic as breathing occupies the brain, freeing the meditator to relax.[xx] So instead of trying to "do nothing"—as meditation appears to an outside observer—a meditator focuses on her breath. Even when we are asleep, our brains are at work: solving problems, hashing out fears.[xxi]

So what do you think happens when we try to rest for an entire day? Our minds begin to wander away from rest. We begin to think about how badly the Camry needs an oil change or that the cell phone bill most certainly is due or that we really ought to e-mail Jeffrey when we get to the office on Monday.

That's not very relaxing, is it?

If you try to do nothing on the Sabbath, then you're probably not going to be very successful.

Remember the Sabbath

But God gives us something on which to focus our attention. Notice the first word of the commandment: *remember* the Sabbath...

In the original Hebrew, the word is *zâkar,* meaning "to mark (so as to be recognized), i.e. to remember"; to be mindful, recount, record.[xxii] So *zâkar* is a command to remember. Remember what, exactly? The original Sabbath, the day in which God rested after creation.

Now, some may say the word *remember* in the commandment means "don't forget" as in, "Don't forget to observe the Sabbath," and in fact the New Living Translation says just that:

> Remember to observe the Sabbath day by
> keeping it holy.

This is a valid argument, but even if it is a correct interpretation, the fourth commandment does directly reference creation in Exodus 20:11:

> For in six days the LORD made the heavens
> and the earth, the sea, and all that is in them,
> but he rested on the seventh day.

So instead of trying to focus on nothing, we should take God's lead and do what He did. While resting, God surveyed His creation. When's the last time you woke up to watch the sunrise? If you're anything like me, you're scrambling just to get to church on time. But we should be imitators of God (Eph. 5:1), surveying His awesome creations. Look no further than the birth of a child.

My daughter was born on Christmas day. They say children are gifts from God, but she was literally our Christmas present. I was elated as the time drew near for her to enter the world. With each of my wife's excruciating contractions, I knew I would soon get to hold my daughter.

Now that she's three, I can barely remember how tiny she was. I see other babies and marvel that she was once that small, that fragile. She came into the world with a full head of hair, a beating heart, and a fresh set of lungs ready to make themselves heard.

Take even the smallest part of the body, like the toe or ear or knee, and examine the skeletal, muscular, cardiovascular, and other systems at work, and it is blatantly obvious that God's creation is good. It is nigh impossible to look at the sunrise over the Atlantic, the star-filled sky, or a newborn child and not proclaim it as good. Out of this realization comes a compulsion to worship the Creator—a compulsion not born of force but of awe.

Taking time to reflect on God's creation means we focus on something beyond ourselves. Our work may seem important. That job or that worry might be commanding our attention. But these things are small compared to God. Remembering the Sabbath, then, is an act of worship, just not in the way you might think of the word.

Get Some Perspective

Worship directs our focus away from ourselves and therefore away from our problems. When we are deliberate about resting, we get several benefits:

- We get some perspective on our situation.

- We realize how small we are.

- We realize a God who created the entire universe has a solution to our problems.

- We realize our to-do lists aren't as important as we thought.

Martha struggled with this problem. Her sister, Mary, wasn't helping Martha cook supper for the guests. Instead she was at the feet of Jesus, listening to His words. Martha became angry, but Jesus told her, "You are worried and upset about many things, but few things are needed—or indeed only one. Mary has chosen what is better, and it will not be taken away from her" (Luke 10:41–42).

Martha was focused on the here and now; Mary was focused on the eternal.

The Sabbath is a reminder that our situation is temporary. God is eternal. When we worship Him, it takes our minds off of dirty dishes and house repair and allows us truly to rest.

Yes, there are things on earth that demand our attention. We still have to shave, and we still have to eat. My advice is this: shift as much of that as you can to other days of the week and allow for one day when you can focus on God.

Now you're ready for better rest. Just don't overlook that one word:

Remember.

Part II

Find Inner Peace

You will keep in perfect peace those whose minds are steadfast, because they trust in you. (Isa. 23:6)

CHAPTER 4

Are You Living Like a Slave?

My chest was heavy.

I wasn't ill. But I wasn't breathing right. The puffs of air came in short bursts.

I had just finished day two of working from dawn until way past dusk. I spent the daylight hours renovating an old building: moving debris, hanging lights, and painting. When the sun set, I got in my truck and drove across town to Tori's Pizzeria, where I made pizza pies all night.

By that second day, I was tired. The chest pain was my body's way of telling me to slow down because my rational mind didn't have the guts to mention it. That night I welcomed my bed and the chance to go to sleep. The next day the pain was gone other than some sore muscles. But I was still fatigued.

It was Sunday, so after church, I sat down on the couch to watch some football like any good American. I didn't intend to fall asleep, but I did. My eyes drooped, and I slowly lost consciousness.

I woke to a sense of euphoria. I was warm, I was comfortable, and I was numb. You'd think I had never napped before in my life. I tried hard not to move because I didn't want the unfeeling to end.

When do we value rest the most? When we don't have the option to rest and when we are beholden to a commitment, a whip, or worse. The same was true with Israel.

You see, the Ten Commandments are recorded twice in the Bible, in Exodus 20 and Deuteronomy 5. The fourth commandment is almost identical in both passages, but Deuteronomy contains an additional phrase:

> Remember that you were slaves in Egypt and that the LORD your God brought you out of there with a mighty hand and an outstretched arm. Therefore the LORD your God has commanded you to observe the Sabbath day. (Deut. 5:15)

That second sentence may seem like a non sequitur, but not from the Hebrew perspective. In Egypt there was no rest. The Israelites worked ruthlessly at the hands of their slave masters, and their lives were constant laboring (Ex. 1:14).

Moses brings this up for two reasons:

- First, to remind Israel that God—and God alone—delivered her from bondage; the Israelites did nothing of their own accord to free themselves from Egypt.

- Second, so they would use the day to commemorate their freedom by resting voluntarily.[xxiii] When Israel was enslaved, they did not have that option.

Once free of Egypt, the Israelites might be tempted to adopt a new master: money, power, or prestige. If they became workaholics to increase their yield—working without ceasing—then they simply would be swapping out one master for another.

The First Steps to Finding Inner Peace

You and I were once slaves too. But we were slaves to something much more dangerous than whips and chains. We were slaves to our sin nature. Sin is our Egypt. And God staged an even greater Exodus for those who believe when He sent His Son to die on the cross. Jesus paid our debts because, just like the Israelites, we were helpless, unable to free ourselves. And "with a mighty hand and an outstretched arm," God freed us from the bondage of sin.

Jesus spoke to this point:

> Very truly I tell you, everyone who sins is a slave to sin. Now a slave has no permanent place in the family, but a son belongs to it

> forever. So if the Son sets you free, you will
> be free indeed. (John 8:34–36)

The first step to finding peace is to allow God to set you free because only a free man can have rest. But we must choose it; that means believing in Jesus and accepting Him as your Savior.

Once you're free, stay free. Don't go back to Egypt. Don't turn to other masters. This is where the Sabbath comes in. Observing the Sabbath does two things: reminds us of our freedom and helps prevent us from taking on new masters. These masters come in many forms: worry, pleasure, money, career.

If you don't have time to devote to Sabbath, then you're probably still living like a slave.

CHAPTER 5

The Real Reason You Don't Have Peace

Though I'm quite ashamed to admit it, for a time I put my hope in things other than Christ.

During my freshman year of college, I got heavy into politics. As the United States was preparing to invade Iraq, I consumed as much political talk as I could. I listened to all of the conservative pundits, gathering mountains of information. I would argue with anyone who was willing about the merits of the conservative agenda. I thought one side was right and one side was wrong. Of course it's not as simple as that.

But as much as I argued and discussed and fought and listened to the Republicans and Democrats, I never really had peace. My heart was still troubled the bad guys believed the way they did and didn't listen to reason. It's safe to say I assimilated politics into my religion.

No matter how much I studied political events, I never really had peace because I never really consulted God. I remember one day watching a town hall meeting on television. A protestor pretending to ask a question instead held up an image of a deformed child. The station quickly cut away to a different camera, but for an instant, the world saw this gruesome sight. The image was barely recognizable as human.

I don't even remember what she was protesting; I have no idea what her point was. But in that moment, I felt tears rolling down my face. I felt hopeless. I had worked so hard to make sure I had all of the answers. But when faced with the picture of a misshapen child, I broke down.

I was out of answers.

I could do nothing but fall to my knees and ask God, "Why? Why is there so much pain? Why is there suffering?"

Then it hit me.

No amount of politicking, arguing, or convincing can change the fact that man is fallen. The only true solution to our problems is to trust in Jesus. That's why I didn't have peace. Even though I was attending a Bible college, I rarely read the Scriptures. I rarely prayed. I was putting my trust in a political ideology instead of in Christ.

Maybe for you it is finances. Or maybe your trust is in human relationships. Whatever it is, if your hope is not in Christ, there will come a day when you run out of answers, and what you thought you could rely upon will let you down. But whatever you are going through, you can have peace.

My Presence Will Go with You

In Exodus, God saved the Israelites from Egypt.

But He didn't stop there. He didn't get them across the Red Sea and say, "See you later. You're on your own now." Instead He gave them the promise of their own land and traveled with them through the desert:

> The LORD replied, "My Presence will go with you, and I will give you rest." (Ex. 33:14)

But do you ever wonder why God didn't lead the children of Israel straight to the Promised Land? Why did they have to go through the desert at all? Had they taken a direct route, they could have arrived at the Promised Land in just a few months rather than forty years.[xxiv]

Here's why: God wanted Israel to learn to trust in Him. He freed the Israelites from their masters, but now they had to rely on a new Master. As one commentator writes:

> [God] tried whether they would trust him, and walk in the law of faith or no, whether they could live from hand to mouth, and ... he tried whether they would serve him, and be always faithful to so good a Master, that provided so well for his servants.[xxv]

The Israelites had no food, so God sent them manna. They had no water, so God gave them some. He reinforced His role as provider so they might rely on Him. The road to the Promised Land wasn't easy, and maybe that's the whole point.

Peace Is Not External

Anyone who tells you turning to Jesus brings a life free of conflict is a liar. We still live in the world; we are still limited by our flesh. The real reason we lack peace is not because we have problems but because we have not surrendered these problems to God. Paul writes, "The mind governed by the flesh is death, but the mind governed by the Spirit is life and peace" (Rom. 8:6). Yet rather than let the Spirit take over, we still hang on to our problems, trying to control them. Trying to provide for ourselves. Therefore we are plagued with anxiety.

But Jesus said not to worry:

> Do not worry about your life, what you will eat or drink; or about your body, what you will wear. Is not life more than food, and the body more than clothes? (Matt. 6:25)

When the fourth commandment tells us to rest from work, it has some implied consequences; it means trusting in God—not in the work of our own hands—to provide. Because time spent in rest is time we could use to earn more money, to provide more income for our families.

Our lives are like wandering journeys through the desert. How then can we rest when we are always in need of water or food and when the desert sun beats down upon us? How can we rest when we have to deal with illness, with the loss of loved ones?

The key is to look forward and remember God's promise. Although life may be rough, we can rest in the fact that God always keeps His word. If we believe in Him, we will have eternal life (John 3:16). And the assurance of eternity gives us peace.

Because, you see, peace is not an external thing. Jesus gave this very message to His disciples to prepare them for His death. Soon they would be separated from their leader and would face many trials. At the conclusion of Jesus' message, He says, "I have told you these things, so that in me you may have peace. In this world you will have trouble. But take heart! I have overcome the world" (John 16:33).

We always have conflict and pain swirling around us. We are always in want of water while in the desert. The key is to trust in Him even when the world doesn't make sense. Why? Because Christ overcame the world.

Do that and He will give you peace.

CHAPTER 6

The Fourth Commandment's Guide to Eternal Life

After twenty-two consecutive hours in the car, I was ready to kill one of my kids.

They were just as stir-crazy as Katie and I, but they had had a full night's rest (even if it was spent hunched over their seats, necks craned in awkward positions). Their restfulness only added to their restlessness. My wife and I, on the other hand, were wiped. We had taken five-hour shifts driving through rain and state after state to get to New Smyrna Beach, Florida. We drove straight through from Norman, Oklahoma, roughly a twenty-four-hour trip.

Yet despite our state of exhaustion, there was an anticipatory giddiness welling inside us as we (seemingly) inched ever closer to our destination. (Not so) strangely, we didn't have this same excitement on the way the back. Geographically the trip was exactly the same length. But psychologically, it felt about twice as long. Why?

On the way there, we had the promise of rest.

The word *vacation* is a cousin to the word *vacate*. Both come from the Latin root *vacare,* meaning to be free from; to be idle.[xxvi] We get to vacate our work responsibilities for a week. We can do what we want, when we want. Ice cream for dinner? You bet. Lying ocean side all day with a crisp paperback in our hands? Check.

On the way back? Not so much. We were returning to work and responsibilities.

Our lives are kind of like a road trip: exciting at times, grueling at others. But just like my family's road trip to Florida, we too have the promise of rest once we reach our destination:

> The promise of entering his rest still stands.
> (Heb. 4:1)

But God's rest is eternal, and there is no return trip. Our journey on earth, though tough at times, is bearable because we have that promise. We toil on earth doing God's work with the promise of eternal rest in the back of our minds. And that makes the whole trip worth the effort.

Everybody Works

But before we can enter God's rest, we must work—just like the commandment reads: "six days you shall labor" (Ex. 20:9a). And make no mistake about it, everybody works. Yes, even your lazy, overweight uncle who spends all day on the couch in front of the television. Even your sister who does nothing but suck on the government teat year after year.

Everybody works. And you do too.

I'm not necessarily talking about physical labor. If I were, then Uncle Bart wouldn't qualify. As we learned in chapter 3, work is not just physical. It is a state of mind. It is a preoccupation. It is a matter of the heart.

If you've been in the church for any period of time, you've likely heard some worship pastor tell you that we were created to worship. It may be trite, but it's true. Because our minds are always running, we must direct our focus on something. Survey what you focus on the most, and that's what you value. Do you spend all day watching television? Chances are you worship television.

The purpose of our lives is the same as the rest of God's creations: to give Him glory. Therefore our work is worship. But we choose whether or not to worship God. We either do the work of the Father or we serve something or someone else. So when examining the fourth commandment in a metaphorical sense, our six days of labor represent our time on earth.

I bet you can guess what the seventh day is.

Our Work on Earth

We will all cease from working one day, but we cannot obtain rest on our own. Eternal rest must come from God. So if we cannot make it to heaven (rest) on our own, how then should we spend our six days on earth? Does it even matter? Read the following excerpt from Revelation:

> There will be no rest day or night for those who worship the beast and its image, or for anyone who receives the mark of its name." This calls for patient endurance on the part of the people of God who keep his commands and remain faithful to Jesus ... Blessed are the dead who die in the Lord from now on ... they will rest from their labor, for their deeds will follow them. (Rev. 14:11–13)

This passage speaks to end times, but it applies in our age too. There is no rest for those who worship anything but the one true God. How we spend our time is important, and this is how we should spend it: keeping God's commands and remaining faithful to Him. This is our work on earth.

But lest you misunderstand me: rest assured, we cannot earn heaven by our work.

Vital Faith

Who then will enter God's rest?

Jesus says that whoever believes in Him will have eternal life (John 3:16). But if you do not do what God commands you to do, do you really believe in Him? Consider this:

> Faith by itself, if it is not accompanied by action, is dead. (James 2:17)

Is dead faith faith?

Therefore belief is essential, but obedience is vital. This concept is easy to understand but not easy to act upon. Taking a twenty-four-hour road trip is a cakewalk compared to some things we have to do for the sake of the cross. Some are called to persecution, some to missionary work overseas, some to sacrifice.

But when tribulations do come, remember God's promise: we shall have rest. That makes the trip so much easier.

What Not to Do

Israel took a trip of its own. God's people were on the precipice of reaching their destination, and they blew it. They had come so far only to let fear rule them at the penultimate hour. Had they only trusted in God, they would have—at long last—had rest. Instead they gave in to fear and turned their backs on the LORD.

After being freed from Egypt, the Israelites had been traveling through the desert for quite a while, and they were tired. God promised them rest in the form of a land of their own where they could settle and live. On the threshold of reaching that Promised Land, Israel sent spies to scout it out.

Problem was, it was filled with big, mean-looking men. After forty days, the spies came back and gave an exaggerated report about how strong the opponent was. Fear entered the hearts of the Israelites, and they cursed Moses and God for leading them all the way through the desert just to be slaughtered by foreigners:

> "If only we had died in Egypt! Or in this wilderness! Why is the LORD bringing us to this land only to let us fall by the sword? Our wives and children will be taken as plunder. Wouldn't it be better for us to go back to Egypt?" And they said to each other, "We should choose a leader and go back to Egypt."
> (Num. 14:1–4)

They were ready to return to the land where they were slaves! In spite of everything the LORD had done for them, they still doubted He could defeat their enemies.

In case you are keeping score, this isn't the only time the Israelites lamented leaving Egypt (Ex. 15:24, 16:2, Num. 21:5, et al.). In all they grumbled ten times (Num. 14:22), but the final straw was when they did not trust God would deliver them the Promised Land.

As a result, God said Israel would wander the desert for forty more years until all of the current generation passed away (except for Caleb and Joshua). In short, they would not enter God's rest (Num. 14:29–30).

Our Work Is Faith Too

If the fourth commandment is a metaphor, then Egypt is too. Turning back to Egypt means turning our backs on God and embracing sin.

God promises us eternal rest, but our job is to believe in that promise, to trust He will provide even when there are giant men standing in the way. Therefore our "work" is simple (but not easy): to sacrifice our own fears and desires and follow Him. In short, to be obedient:

> Today, if only you would hear his voice, "Do not harden your hearts as you did at Meribah, as you did that day at Massah in the wilderness, where your ancestors tested me; they tried me, though they had seen what I did. For forty years I was angry with that generation; I said, 'They are a people whose hearts go astray, and they have not known my ways.' So I declared on oath in my anger, 'They shall never enter my rest.'" (Ps. 95:7–11)

We enter God's rest by obedience to Him.

> There remains, then, a Sabbath-rest for the
> people of God; for anyone who enters God's
> rest also rests from their works, just as God
> did from his. Let us, therefore, make every
> effort to enter that rest, so that no one will
> perish by following their example of
> disobedience. (Heb. 4:9–11)

This is where faith comes in.

You see, Israel couldn't see the end game. They didn't know
how God was going to defeat their enemies, so they did not
believe.

And it shouldn't even be that hard to believe—especially for
the Israelites, who witnessed the plagues, the Passover, and
the parting of the Red Sea.

The God who created heaven and earth, the God who
brought us out of Egypt, who saved us from our sins when we
did not deserve to be saved, can follow through on His mea-
sly promise to take you to heaven and restore you. I don't
mean to be sacrilegious, but saving us and bringing us to
heaven is nothing for God. It's simple! Do you think anything
is hard for God?

There is one thing: watching humans in bondage—especially
those who voluntarily return.

God wants us to rest. The fourth commandment makes that
abundantly clear. This commandment has practical implications in that it is good for the body, but how much more important is rest for the soul? If you rest your body, you get

tired again the next day, but the rest God offers is everlasting.

And the hour of eternal rest is near. Don't give in to fear and turn your back on God. Persevere in your faith, and you will be richly rewarded. Remember the words of Jesus: "Come to me, all you who are weary and burdened, and I will give you rest" (Matt. 11:28).

Seek the rest that God provides, and you will never be weary again.

Part III

Strengthen Your Faith

These people come near to me with their mouth and honor me with their lips, but their hearts are far from me. Their worship of me is based on merely human rules they have been taught. (Isa. 29:13)

CHAPTER 7

Don't Be Duped by This Sabbath Myth

Before we move forward, let's get one thing straight: the Sabbath takes place on Saturday. It always has, and it always will.

But the Sabbath is not just on Saturday. It, quite literally, is Saturday. It may not be so obvious in our language, because in English the day is named after the planet Saturn. But look at many other languages and you will see that the word for Saturday and Sabbath are the same.

In Spanish, *sábado* (the same in Portuguese).

In Italian, *sabato*.

In Croatian, *subota*.

So to try to separate Saturday and the Sabbath is impossible. Yet that is exactly what many Christians do. It is a great myth spread throughout the Christian culture that Sunday is the Sabbath. That's like saying that Wednesday is the Thursday. Or forty is the new thirty. It doesn't make sense. So don't be duped; there is no Scripture in which Jesus commanded New Covenant people to observe Sunday over Saturday.

Tenuous Footing

But for the longest time I was duped.

You see, I have been in church since I was born. Sunday comes. I am there. In the pew. In the seat. Standing. Singing. Clapping.

Listening, praying, eating flesh, and drinking blood.

Crying.

I do all the right things on Sunday. That makes me a good Christian, and that means I am going to heaven, right?

It is easy for us to fall into this kind of thinking—that devotion on Sunday equates to following God's law. Turns out my righteous footing may be more tenuous than I thought, especially considering that the Sabbath—beginning with the day God rested—is Saturday, the seventh day.

Three Reasons for the Shift to Sunday

So how did Sunday come to be the "Sabbath" for Christians? I have identified three reasons (though I am sure there are more).

1. Jesus rose from the dead on a Sunday.

The most important event in the Bible happened the day after the Sabbath, "The first day of the week." See Luke 24:1-8.

2. Pentecost took place on a Sunday.

Pentecost—the day God poured the out the Holy Spirit on mankind—is another pivotal moment for Christ followers (Acts 2:1-41). The word means "fiftieth day," and it is the Greek term for the Jewish Festival of Weeks.[xxvii] The name is fitting because Old Testament law prescribes that the festival take place "seven full weeks" from "the day after the Sabbath" of the Offering of the Firstfruits (Lev. 23:15)—the day after the Sabbath, of course, being Sunday. So seven times seven plus one equals fifty.

3. The Council of Laodicea in AD 364 formally established Sunday as "The Lord's Day" in Canon 29.

> Christians must not judaize by resting on the Sabbath, but must work on that day, rather honouring the Lord's Day; and, if they can, resting then as Christians. But if any shall be found to be judaizers, let them be anathema from Christ.[xxviii]

Judaizing—trying to justify oneself before God by adhering to Jewish law—had become such a problem that the Christian establishment made a rule against using Saturday as the Sabbath. But do you see what the council members did? They did not dispute that the Sabbath is Saturday. They simply said that the fourth commandment does not apply to Christians.

It is an irony that the council rejected Saturday in response to judaizers because now we do the same thing with Sunday. We think going to church and being good on Sunday is grounds on which we can stand before God and that we can judge others who do not do these things.

Sunday is not unimportant; it is just not as important as you thought.

Yet I am not advocating that we observe Saturday over Sunday. That's up to you. Which day you choose actually is irrelevant. God's way more concerned with your heart than with the calendar.

Besides that, by our clocks the Sabbath actually spans two days; Judaism recognizes the Sabbath as beginning at sundown on Friday. Perhaps the tradition originates with the creation narrative:

> God saw all that he had made, and it was
> very good. And there was evening, and there
> was morning —the sixth day. (Gen. 1:31)

The Scriptures list evening before morning, insinuating it occurred first.

Observe It for the Lord

Don't get caught up in specific days. There is nothing magical about Saturday or Sunday. Not everyone has the luxury of being off work on the weekend, but do not feel guilty:

> Therefore do not let anyone judge you by what you eat or drink, or with regard to a religious festival, a New Moon celebration or a Sabbath day. (Col. 2:16)

God is your judge, not man. If you work on both Saturday and Sunday, do not forsake gathering with other believers. Pick another day. But we would do well to remember that God wants all of us, not just one-seventh. Paul addresses this very issue:

> One person regards one day above another, another regards every day alike. Each person must be fully convinced in his own mind. He who observes the day, observes it for the Lord. (Rom. 14:9)

Remember, God knows your heart. So if you are going to observe the "Sabbath," do it for the Lord. Otherwise, what's the point?

CHAPTER 8

Four Sabbath Mistakes that Make You Sound Like a Pharisee

Misunderstanding the fourth commandment will ruin your religion.

At best you'll be ignorant. At worst, a Pharisee.

Sometimes the best way to strengthen your faith is by learning from others' spiritual screw-ups. Here are four mistakes to avoid lest you run the risk of sounding (or looking) like a Pharisee.

1. Putting the Fourth Commandment ahead of People

The Pharisees prohibited healing on the Sabbath because it was considered "work." Ridiculous, I know. All three synoptic gospels record instances in which Jesus healed on the Sabbath to the chagrin of the religious crowd.

My favorite line from these stories is, "Which is lawful on the Sabbath: to do good or to do evil, to save life or to kill?" (Mark 3:4).

Jesus has a way of making things so obvious.

And although it is obvious, I must confess I have put the fourth commandment ahead of people. In my zeal to please God (or was it laziness?), I chose rest over helping someone out. I had the opportunity to help someone move on a Sunday but chose not to because it was my day of rest.

Although not as extreme of an example as that of the Pharisees, I definitely missed the point of the commandment. We tend to look at commandments as existing in a vacuum. Yet the law must be viewed as a whole (more on this in chapter 10).

Think about the irony here. It seems most of the conflicts that arose between Jesus and the Pharisees in regard to the Sabbath was because of healing. But what is the purpose of the Sabbath? An undeniable component is for physical restoration; in other words, it is for healing. As noted by one commentator, "The sabbath was instituted for the benefit of man, that he might refresh and renew his body, fatigued and worn by six days' labour, with the restful calm of the seventh."[xxix]

Even more ironic is that because Jesus healed and restored life, they wanted to take away His (Matt. 12:9–14). But was their problem really the healing? Or was it that they were worried about losing religious authority? Healing was just a metaphor. You see, Jesus could heal physical ailments, which led people to believe in Him, but He could also heal spiritual ailments (i.e., forgive sin). For sure, the Pharisees were offended at the rule-breaking, but they were far more concerned with hanging on to their power.

Jesus says, "The Sabbath was made for man" (Mark 2:27). In doing so, He expresses, "God's purpose in establishing the seventh day as a period of joy and refreshment."[xxx] God created a day of rest for our benefit. Putting the Sabbath ahead of the well-being of others bastardizes the commandment. Don't do it, or you'll look like a Pharisee.

2. Not Working on the Sabbath (in Certain Situations)

If you don't think public speaking is hard work, you probably haven't done it lately.

I recently gave a ten-minute software demo to a group of one hundred people. Afterward, I was exhausted. I know not everyone who speaks in public gets as anxious as I do, but I know it's hard work.

Have you been to church recently? See how the preacher gets worked up—sweating, pacing, raising his voice? He's definitely laboring up there. And Jesus taught on the Sabbath too (Luke 13:10). Maybe you don't agree that teaching qualifies as work. Still, there are other biblical examples of innocent Sabbath violation. Here's one:

> Haven't you read in the Law that the priests on Sabbath duty in the temple desecrate the Sabbath and yet are innocent? I tell you that something greater than the temple is here. (Matt. 12:5)

This example falls under the Old Covenant. Jesus says the priests on temple duty violate the Sabbath. How? By working. If you think public speaking is tiring, try slaughtering a lamb. I bet those Levites slept well on Saturday night.

Jesus gave the Pharisees this example from their own playbook in response to their assertion the disciples were working by picking grain (Matt. 12:2). You see, He didn't need to debate whether the disciples were working. Why? Because it didn't matter.

There are times in our lives when it is essential to work on the Sabbath. Sick people need someone to take care of them on Saturdays and Sundays too. We need police on the weekends. And there are times when we have to work extra hard just to be able to feed our kids.

What about physical labor? If I run a few miles on the Sabbath, is that work? Some would say yes. What if I run one mile? What if I walk that mile? What if I walk half a mile?

Where do we draw the line? These are exactly the types of questions the Pharisees tried to answer. But they were focusing on the wrong things. Rather than asking, "Am I working?" We should ask, "Why am I working?"

If I run out of a sense of obligation or to earn money, then am I really honoring God? If I run because I want a beautiful bod (hypothetically—I know I already have one), then I turn the act of running into a god, whereby I worship at the altar of beauty.

But maybe I just want to run on the Sabbath because it clears my head, it makes me feel better, I will be better focused in church, or I want to live a healthy lifestyle. Rather than asking, "What?" we must ask, "Why?"

Why are you working? Is it for more money? To get ahead? Or is your motive something for which God would count you blameless?

3. Forgetting Jesus Is Lord of the Sabbath

Without Jesus, the Sabbath is meaningless. His physical healing on earth was a representation of the spiritual healing He would provide by His death. He paved the way so we could have eternal rest. Jesus is the authority on the Sabbath, not man:

> The Son of Man is Lord of the Sabbath.
> (Matt. 12:8)

Right before Jesus said this, He quoted the Old Testament prophet Hosea, "I desire mercy, not sacrifice" (6:6). In chapter 2, I referred to the Sabbath as a tithe of time. Yet in quoting the prophet, Jesus affirms that God would rather us be merciful to others than to sacrifice our time.

We should not try to please other Christians, our pastor, or a denomination. Instead we should try to please God. Observing the Sabbath but neglecting to acknowledge Jesus makes you look like a Pharisee. Jesus is the one who makes rest possible. Yes, the Sabbath was made for man, but who made the Sabbath?

4. Making Up Your Own Sabbath Rules

The Pharisees added to the fourth commandment quite a bit: mat carrying, healing, how far one could walk. In doing so, they missed the point. They knew what the intent of the law was, but they didn't really care about that. Instead they cared about being legalistic.

That's why when Jesus said, "Not one of you keeps the law," it was particularly stinging (John 7:19). They had hung their hat on following the law, and they were the righteous ones because they kept it to the letter. All the rest were "sinners." (Of course, it was easy for them to keep the law because they interpreted it.) But God never meant for it to be illegal to heal someone on the Sabbath:

If any of you has a sheep and it falls into a pit
on the Sabbath, will you not take hold of it
and lift it out? (Matt. 12:11)

He made the teachers of the law look silly. How much more
important is a man than a sheep? God gave us the Sabbath so
we would have refreshment and regeneration, not for the
burden of more rules and regulations.

The Pharisees added to God's law to judge others and justify
themselves before Him. Self-justification was never possible
before, but now that Christ is raised, we have even less of an
excuse.

Don't make up silly Sabbath rules so you keep the commandment extra good. If you observe the commandment, do
it out of love and respect for the Father, not to feel good
about yourself and especially not to judge others. God is our
judge, not man.

Avoid These Four Mistakes

So what do these four things have in common? The first two
reflect selfishness: putting our desires and comfort ahead of
others and ahead of a higher calling. The last two reflect
pride: not ceding authority and adding to the law.

If you act selfishly or out of pride, you may be able to rest
physically, but spiritually you will be in conflict with God. So
even if you're not concerned about sounding like a Pharisee,

be sure to avoid these mistakes so you might please our heavenly Father.

CHAPTER 9

Learn This One Thing and Your Faith Will Be Light Years Ahead of Most Christians

No, faith is not a competition. But it seems as I read blogs, talk to people, and watch television that so many people struggle with this one issue. If the apostle Peter did, anyone can. I know I did (and still do).

I had been studying the fourth commandment for months, asking myself, *Is it still relevant?* One morning I had a breakthrough. I got up early on a Saturday morning to try to get in some writing before the kids woke up. I was beating my head against this issue of Old Testament law and New Covenant people specifically in the context of the fourth commandment.

At some point I migrated to the bathroom floor, because my boys woke up and occupied the living room. So there I sat, my tailbone asleep, laptop in lap, thinking, praying, reading, writing, deleting, retyping, and deleting again.

I began to read Acts 10, in which Peter receives a vision from God to "kill and eat" animals unclean by the standard of Mosaic Law (v. 13). After reading the story, I read through some commentaries on the text, and I stumbled upon this quotation from Albert Barnes in his *Notes on the New Testament* that changed my view on Old Testament Law:

> Once the barrier was removed that separated the Jews and Gentiles, all the laws which were founded on such a distinction, and which were framed to keep up such a distinction, passed away of course.

In retrospect it should have been obvious, but I know I was not alone in my ignorance. I know many Christians struggle with this issue, especially in regard to the fourth commandment.

What's So Special about the Ten Commandments?

But, but, but … it's one of the Ten Commandments!

That's one of the most common arguments for following the fourth commandment. Well, I'm here to ask to the unaskable: What's so special about the Ten Commandments?

Excuse me while I dodge lightning.

Am I being sacrilegious? Maybe. But before I continue, let me assure you of one thing: I believe there is an ultimate moral law. And I believe God alone is the ultimate moral lawgiver.

So please don't hear that I don't believe God has established a moral law. My point is that the Ten Commandments are only valid to the Christian inasmuch as they are moral.

Old timers in the evangelical world love to point out to youngsters that Leviticus 19:28 says not to get tattoos. They keep these Bible bullets in their belts ready to be fired at any moment at the "heathen" who is considering inking up. Yet these same people conveniently neglect dozens of other Levitical laws they break every day. Here are just a few examples:

1. Don't clip the sides of your beard (Lev. 19:27).

2. Don't eat bloody steak (Lev. 19:26).

3. Don't wear polyester and cotton blended shirts (Lev. 19:19).

That, my friends, is hypocrisy. It is judgmental. It is judiazing. The sad thing is that these comments reveal way more about the faith of the criticizer than about the one who has a tattoo on his body. The judaizer is deceived.

So why is it okay to cut your beard but not okay to get tattoos? Why is it okay to get tattoos but not okay to break the Sabbath? This is always where the "it's one of the Ten Commandments" argument comes in. So again I ask, what's so special about the Ten Commandments? The Scripture says he who breaks one law breaks the whole law (Jam. 2:10). That verse does not single out the Ten Commandments.

This subject merits its own book entirely, and I'm sure there are plenty of great ones already written. So here is the abbreviated version: Old Testament law was originally intended for the Hebrew people. It serves multiple functions, but two central purposes are these: to set Israel apart from other nations (Lev. 20:26) and for moral reasons. The issue is much more complex, but that's a good starting point. Tattoos? Founded upon a distinction. Beards? Distinction. Murder? Moral. Ceasing work on the Sabbath? Read on.

Is It Still Relevant?

The word *Sabbath* appears ninety-six times in the Old Testament.[xxxi] That might not seem like that much, but consider this: the words *repent* and *forgive* (or any form of these words) combined only appear eighty-three times in the same space.

I am not arguing that the Sabbath concept is more important than repentance and forgiveness. Clearly not. But when I finally read through the entire Old Testament, I was struck by how many times the Scriptures mention the Sabbath.

Our (largely Christian) culture tells us the fourth commandment is irrelevant. Yet we don't think twice about the other nine. Of course we shouldn't murder. Nor should we steal or have other gods. But in case you haven't heard, Jesus kind of changed the game. He did not "come to abolish [the Law and the Prophets] but to fulfill them" (Matt. 5:17).

So does that make the commandment irrelevant? Absolutely not! The commandment's primary purpose was to distinguish Jews from Gentiles. Yet there are elements of morality embedded in its core. After all, the first Sabbath took place before the nation of Israel even existed (Gen. 2:1–3). There were no Jews or Gentiles on that day.

Three Moral Issues in the Fourth Commandment

So here are three ways in which neglecting to observe the Sabbath can lead to moral deficiency:

1. It results in abuse of your body.

God gave the Sabbath in part for our benefit. The body needs refreshment; it's not made to run seven days a week. Failing to rest from work leads to burnout and over time, self-abuse. First Corinthians 6:19 says our bodies are temples. We house the Holy Spirit. Neglecting to take care of that temple is a mistake.

2. It disrespects the sacrifice Jesus endured to set us free.

Israel's narrative was the Exodus from Egypt. Our freedom comes via the cross. When once we were sentenced to death,

Jesus stood in our place that we might have eternal rest. Failure to cease work means taking for granted the sacrifice that makes rest possible at all.

3. It demonstrates a lack of faith that God will provide.

Sabbath violation can be symptomatic of a serious ill. It reveals a deep-seated disbelief that God can really provide for our needs. And I'm not just talking about physical needs. We can't earn salvation by works. We know this intellectually, yet our sense of inadequacy drives us to try to earn God's favor.

Remember what Jesus said to Satan when He was starving in the desert? Quoting Deuteronomy He said, "Man shall not live on bread alone, but on every word that comes from the mouth of God" (Matt. 4:4). The Sabbath is an invitation to acknowledge the fact that not only will God provide our physical needs, but He will save us from sin, just as He promised.

One story exemplifies all three of these principles. When the Israelites escaped Egypt, God sent manna to feed His people while in the wilderness. Every morning like dew (Num. 11:9) the heavenly bread appeared on the ground. Every morning, that is, but on Saturday.

On the sixth day, the people were to gather enough for two days because the seventh day was "to be a day of sabbath rest, a holy sabbath to the LORD" (Ex. 16:23). Keep in mind that this occurred before God gave Moses the Ten Commandments. But the day of rest was for the LORD; it allowed the Israelites to focus on their God. The LORD provided twice as much on the sixth day so they didn't have to worry about food on the seventh (Ex. 16:29). God was their provider. The Sabbath served as a reminder.

As recently freed slaves, the idea of rest was foreign to the Israelites. Resting not only allowed them to praise the infinite God but also to reflect on the freedom He provided. In the hands of the Egyptians, they did not have the option to rest. The Sabbath was a commemoration of their freedom.

Resting also provided the people much-needed refreshment. Not only did they not gather manna, but no one even left his tent (Ex. 16:29–30).

We see in this narrative that the Sabbath transcends Judaism. It addresses both our physical and spiritual needs. So even if the fourth commandment isn't binding to New Covenant believers, the principles behind it are sound.

Yet even knowing all of these things, it is easy to slip back into a mind-set of trying to justify oneself before God. It's just not going to happen. The only way to salvation is in justification by faith through grace (Eph. 2:8–9). I don't know about you, but I often regress into this self-justification mind-set. And if that doesn't make you feel any better, this should: it happened to the father of the church, the one Jesus called "rock."

Peter's Vision and Where He Went Wrong

Let's go back to that strange dream Simon Peter had. You know, the one in which a giant quilt filled with creepy crawlies and other disgusting animals was lowered from the sky to the earth. After it landed, God told Peter to kill the animals and eat them. Delicious.

Of course Peter complained:

> "Surely not, Lord!" Peter replied. "I have never eaten anything impure or unclean."
> (Acts 10:14)

Like many visions in the Bible, this one is a metaphor. And I've got news for you; we are the disgusting animals in Peter's dream. Those "unclean" animals are the Gentiles. Fortunately God said, "Do not call anything impure that God has made clean" (Acts 10:15). You know how He made us clean? By the blood of Christ.

The Old Covenant was all about cleanliness. There are entire chapters devoted to how to deal with mold, leprosy, discharges, zits, and other really gross stuff. The Jews were not to be defiled by these things lest they be unclean before God. We Gentiles were just plain nasty to the Jews.

But Jesus came to earth and fulfilled the Law (Matt. 5:17). What does that mean? For the answer, I direct you to New Testament scholar R. T. France:

> The whole Old Testament, the law as well as
> the prophets, pointed forward to what Jesus
> has now brought into being.*xxxii*

For just one example of this, let's go back to when God first called Abram. Here's what He said: "All peoples on earth will be blessed through you" (Gen. 12:3b).

He's talking about His Son, Jesus! God used the people of Israel, descended from Abraham, as a vehicle by which to deliver the Messiah. Jesus came and gave Himself up as a sacrifice for our sins, fulfilling the Old Covenant. The kingdom is now open to anyone, Jew or Gentile, who believes in Christ. This is the realization Peter had, the vision God gave to him on the rooftop that day:

> I now realize how true it is that God does not
> show favoritism but accepts from every
> nation the one who fears him and does what
> is right. (Acts 10:34–35)

Peter and subsequently Paul began to take the Word to the Gentiles, converting them in droves to Christ. Now everyone was content; they were just one big happy family of humanity, right?

Antioch, We Have a Problem

Not so fast.

You see, at this point, God tore down the barrier between the Jew and Gentile. But it wasn't long before Jewish believers began trying to tell Gentiles how to live for Christ. Whether with the right intention or not, they tried to force Jewish customs on the Gentiles and get them to forsake their own customs:

> Then some of the believers who belonged to the party of the Pharisees stood up and said, "The Gentiles must be circumcised and required to keep the Law of Moses." (Acts 15:5)

The judaizers obviously did not understand the full meaning of Peter's vision. And even Peter himself struggled with it. Paul recounts in Galatians how Peter backslid into a habit of separating himself from Gentiles because he feared the circumcision group (2:12). This group was trying to rely on their heritage to save them. But Paul had this to say:

> All who rely on the works of the law are under a curse, as it is written: "Cursed is everyone who does not continue to do everything written in the Book of the Law." Clearly no one who relies on the law is justified before God, because "the righteous will live by faith." (Gal. 3:10-11)

So it takes faith to be right with God. Which makes the whole of Old Testament law, including the fourth commandment irrelevant, right?

How to Break the Fourth Commandment

Wrong again.

If nothing more, Old Testament law merits study for its historicity alone. But even more, studying the law and reading those boring chapters in Leviticus reveals to us who God is— not that He's boring but meticulous and detail-oriented. Each word reveals to us a bit more about God's character: what He values, His personality (because God is a personal God), His love, attention to detail, and more.

Again, from a Christian perspective, the law applies where it has to do with morality. The law shows us that we could not possibly keep it all, which is why we need grace:

> A person is justified by faith apart from the works of the law. (Rom. 3:28)

The opposite of grace is works. This is where Peter got into trouble, and it is one way a New Covenant believer can break the fourth commandment: attempting to use the law to justify oneself rather than relying on the blood of Jesus for salvation.

This, of course, applies to all laws, but it is especially tricky with the fourth commandment because it contains elements both of Jewish distinction and of morality. But if you can understand that distinguishing laws were fulfilled by the resurrection of Christ, then your faith will be light years ahead of the average Christian's.

CHAPTER 10

Warning: This Chapter Might Make Pharisees Look Dumb

If you are a Pharisee, you might want to stop reading now; I don't want to hurt your feelings. If you are a judaizer, a christianizer, a Sadducee, or a legalist, close your laptop lid. Put down your Kindle or your iPad. I'd like to stay friends.

But if you keep reading, you have been warned: you might feel like a fool after reading this chapter. Trust me. These words come from a reformed Pharisee.

My dad used to call me a legalist. And I don't begrudge him this. In fact, I should thank him because he was right. And he opened my eyes to many things I could not understand on my own. He didn't do it in a mean-spirited way, but I really was a letter-of-the-law kind of guy. My parents routinely suggested I should become a lawyer because I read everything literally and followed the rules exactly. (You didn't want to play board games with me.)

Here's a confession between you and me: I still struggle with it.

But the more I study the Scriptures and the more I ponder God's words, works, motives, and laws, the more I realize how much I was truly missing by focusing on the letter of the law instead of the intent. Make no bones about it: God's law is just. God's law is holy (Rom. 7:12). But there is an hierarchy whereby following one law might mean breaking another.

So if you're a Pharisee like I was, take especial note of what I'm about to say.

Positive vs. Negative

Now a veteran of parenting (I just signed a contract extension for a fourth child), I can tell you one thing that I have learned: There are two types of commands: positive commands and negative commands. A negative command tells one what not to do:

"Don't yell in the car."

"Okay."

Child begins to sing very loudly.

"Don't sing so loudly."

"Okay."

Child begins to bang Spiderman against the cup holder.

"For heaven's sake, don't do that!"

A positive command tells one what to do:

"Please be quiet."

Do you see how one positive command implies all three of the negative commands? It is much clearer and more succinct.

Although the fourth commandment contains both types, the negatives serve to clarify the positives. The essence of the commandment lies in its positive aspects: "Remember the Sabbath by keeping it holy" (Ex. 20:8) and "Six days you shall labor and do all your work" (Ex. 20:9).

God commands us to *do* something as opposed to *not doing* something. Failing to pick up on this, the Pharisees instead focused on what not to do on the Sabbath:

You cannot heal.

You cannot pick grain.

You cannot carry your mat.

You cannot walk a certain distance.

Do you see how backward this is? Let's assume for a moment that the Pharisees made these rules out of a genuine interest in honoring God. Even so, adding to the law is still wrong. They made prohibitions that may or not cause people to honor God. Let's face it: it would be extremely easy for me to abstain from healing, walking, picking grain, and carrying my mat yet still dishonor God.

The teachers of the law totally missed the point because they did not understand the intent of the commandment. They were focusing on the negative instead of the positive.

Now I know what you're thinking: eight out of the ten commandments are negative commands. (Honor your mother and father is the other positive.) So I must not know what I'm talking about, right?

The Least-Understood Commandment

Yes, it is true that much of Old Testament law, including the Ten Commandments, tells Israel what not to do. But Jesus—like He had a knack for doing—turned all of this on its head. You see, the fourth commandment is the most overlooked because it is the least understood. The other nine are much easier to understand—on the surface.

"You shall not murder" (Ex. 20:13) is pretty straightforward right? But then Jesus comes along and says:

> You have heard that it was said to the people long ago, "You shall not murder, and anyone who murders will be subject to judgment." But I tell you that anyone who is

angry with a brother or sister will be subject to judgment. Again, anyone who says to a brother or sister, "Raca," is answerable to the court. (Matt. 5:21–22)

Jesus equates hate to murder. And the book of 1 John puts it more plainly when it reads, "Anyone who hates a brother or sister is a murderer" (3:15).

What about adultery? That's cut and dry: do not have sex with someone other than your spouse. But then Jesus had to go and say, "Anyone who looks at a woman lustfully has already committed adultery with her in his heart" (Matt. 5:28).

Those two statements don't allow the commandments to fit into the neat little compartments to which we try to isolate them. Do you see what Jesus does here?

He overturns the assumptions the teachers of law made about God's Law. Who would have thought that when the Scriptures say "Thou shall not murder," it also means "thou shall not hate"?

Therefore, even with the obvious laws, we cannot rely solely on the negative command. Sounds like what we need here is a positive command or two.

The Fourth Is Not the Greatest

Luckily for us, Jesus gave us those two commands. Someone had the nerve to ask Him which command was the greatest. Jesus said:

> Love the Lord your God with all your heart and with all your soul and with all your strength. (Matt. 22:37)

Notice He didn't pick any of the ten. He picked a positive command—one that tells us to do something: love God with everything we have in us. And He didn't stop there. The questioner didn't ask what the two greatest commandments are, but Jesus gave him a second one nonetheless:

> Love your neighbor as yourself. (Matt. 22:39)

Did His answer surprise the people? It probably surprised the Pharisees. And in case you're wondering, Jesus didn't just make up these commandments (although He could have, being God and all). Both are part of the Pentateuch—the first five books of the Bible (Deut. 6:5, Lev. 19:18)—so the Pharisees would have had them memorized.

Jesus did not shy away from this question, and in answering it, He set up a hierarchy of the Law. It means that when there is a conflict between commands, we choose the greater of two goods.

If you love, that means you don't hate. That's why Jesus said the two greatest commandments were to love God and love your neighbor as yourself. That covers everything. What about murder? If you love, you don't murder. What about coveting? If you love your neighbor, you won't covet his possessions. Idolatry? If you love God, you won't put anything before Him.

Positive commands are much more valuable than negative because they tell us how to behave. If you tell someone not to do something, he knows what is not okay to do, but he still has to occupy that space with something. He has to do, think, or believe something instead.

What an embarrassment this must have been to the Pharisees, who made it illegal to heal on the Sabbath. What do the greatest commandments say? If healing really is "work," then it is still okay to heal on the Sabbath if it means in doing so we are fulfilling the greatest commandment. As Jesus said:

> If a boy can be circumcised on the Sabbath so that the law of Moses may not be broken, why are you angry with me for healing a man's whole body on the Sabbath? Stop judging by mere appearances, but instead judge correctly. (John 7:23–24)

If you were sick and dying, would you care on which day of the week someone healed you? I thought not.

So if you want to truly follow the fourth (or any other) commandment, ask yourself these two questions: Would my actions reflect a supreme love for my God? Would my actions (or inaction) mean loving my neighbor as I love myself? These questions are much harder to ask than to say, "Did I earn a paycheck today? Nope. I just followed the fourth commandment."

Allow me to give you one example of this principle from Scripture.

The Good Samaritan

This story does not specifically involve the fourth commandment, but its implications are the similar. The Good Samaritan is a story I didn't understand for a long time. I'm sure there are still nuances and contexts I don't truly get, but I have a much better grasp on it than I once did.

I used to think it was just about some stuck-up guys who didn't care about a man who was clearly in need and about a kind soul who helped out. And while that is the core of the story, there is one thing we need to note here: The stuck-up men were priests in the temple. These weren't regular schmoes just walking by. As such they were actually observing Levitical law by not going near the man:

> A priest must not make himself ceremonially
> unclean for any of his people who die, except
> for a close relative. (Lev. 21:1b–2a)

Now, they didn't know for sure if the man was dead, but they couldn't take the risk of being unclean. Uncleanliness was a serious deal, especially for a priest or a Levite. It would have been risky and possibly damaging for these Jews to go out of their way to help out. Yet that is exactly what we are supposed to do.

God's Laws Are Not in a Vacuum

We cannot approach the Law as though each is in a vacuum. Each is related to one another, and they all point back to who God is, how we should relate to Him, and how He wants us to relate to others.

The priest and Levite should have violated the law to serve a greater good: saving another man's life. If they were beat up and left for dead, do you think they would have been all that concerned with laws of cleanliness?

Remember what Jesus said:

> If any of you has a sheep and it falls into a pit on the Sabbath, will you not take hold of it and lift it out? How much more valuable is a person than a sheep! Therefore it is lawful to do good on the Sabbath. (Matt. 12:11–12)

If you want to become a Pharisee, focus on the lesser commandments at the expense of the greatest commandment. But focus on the greatest commandments and God will take care of everything else.

It's All about Your Heart

T hink of the last time you felt really rested.

For some that might be years ago. For others that might be yesterday.

Whenever it was, I bet it was after a period of work or stress. That God rested on the Seventh day and not on the first is no coincidence. God gave us the Sabbath as a gift: a time to recharge, to reflect, and to rest. It is a time when we can stand back, be still, and know God is God.

The Sabbath brings us rest, but it is also a symbol—a reminder of the eternal rest that is to come. It is a reminder that once we were slaves, but now we can rest in the freedom of the blood of Christ.

But as much as we are commanded to rest, we are also commanded to work—not out of obligation but out of a love for the Father who has set us free.

Paul says we should become slaves to righteousness (Rom. 6:19). The truth is we all serve someone or something, even if we are not aware of it. Look at how you spend your time, both on and off the Sabbath, and it will give you insight into what you truly value.

But in your service to God, do not become fixated and judgmental with regard to rules. God wants us to love Him with everything in our being as He loves us. And in our love for Him, we love others, realizing we cannot truly love the Father yet hate the Father's children.

> Remember the Sabbath day by keeping it holy. Six days you shall labor and do all your work, but the seventh day is a sabbath to the LORD your God. On it you shall not do any work, neither you, nor your son or daughter, nor your male or female servant, nor your animals, nor any foreigner residing in your towns. For in six days the LORD made the heavens and the earth, the sea, and all that is in them, but he rested on the seventh day. Therefore the LORD blessed the Sabbath day and made it holy. (Ex. 20:8–11)

Never Trust Theological Advice

I've spent many hours in research and prayer in preparation for this book. I hope that was apparent.

But although I worked hard to provide you guidance, you should never trust theological advice without vetting it in Scripture. There are too many people deceiving the masses with false words. I have not intentionally misrepresented the gospel in any way, but there is only One who is infallible.

My challenge to you is this: grab your Bible and read through these concepts.

Then go to http://www.andrewgilmore.net/p/iv.html and let me know what helped change your thinking about the Sabbath and which things you disagree with. I look forward to hearing from you.

Also, don't forget to sign up for exclusive content at http://bit.ly/1ia5mRZ. It's totally free, and gives you access to material I don't publish anywhere else. (Consider it our little secret.)

Rest well.

Endnotes

[i] Frank B. Minirth et al., *Beating Burnout: Balanced Living for Busy People* (New York: Inspirational Press, 1997), 15.

[ii] Ibid., 14–15.

[ii] Ibid., 14–15.

[iii] Sabine Bährer-Kohler, ed., *Burnout for Experts Prevention in the Context of Living and Working* (Boston, MA: Springer US, 2013), Ebook edition, 24.

[iv] Victor P. Hamilton, *The Book of Genesis* (Grand Rapids: William B. Eerdmans, 1990), 171.

[v] Mark Buchanan, *The Rest of God: Restoring Your Soul by Restoring Sabbath* (Nashville, TN: W Pub. Group, 2006), 23.

[vi] Minirth, *Beating Burnout*, 15.

[vii] James Strong, "The New Strong's Expanded Dictionary of the Words in the Hebrew Bible." In *The New Strong's Exhaustive Concordance of the Bible*, Expanded ed. (Nashville, TN: Thomas Nelson Inc., 2010), 271.

[viii] G. Tyler Miller and Scott Spoolman, *Living in the Environment: Concepts, Connections, and Solutions*, 16th ed. (Pacific Grove, CA: Brooks/Cole, 2009), 305.

[ix] Joan Borysenko, *Inner Peace for Busy People: 52 Simple Strategies for Transforming Your Life* (Carlsbad, CA: Hay House, 2001), 4.

[x] "National Sleep Foundation White Paper," National Sleep Foundation, accessed November 1, 2013, http://www.sleepfoundation.org/article/white-papers/national-sleep-foundation-white-paper, 7th paragraph.

[xi] "The Science of Sleep," BBC, accessed November 1, 2013, http://www.bbc.co.uk/science/humanbody/sleep/articles/whatissleep.shtml.

[xii] Brian C. Tefft, "Asleep at the Wheel: The Prevalence and Impact of Drowsy Driving," AAA Foundation for Traffic Safety, last modi-

fied November 2010, accessed November 1, 2013,
https://www.aaafoundation.org/sites/default/files/2010DrowsyDrivin
gReport_1.pdf, 1.

[xiii] Borysenko, 48.

[xiv] George A. Buttrick et al., *Interpreter's Dictionary of the Bible: an Illustrated Encyclopedia, Vol. 4* (Nashville, TN: Abingdon, 1962), 135.

[xv] Strong, 182.

[xvi] Raymond A. Serway, Jerry S. Faughn, and Chris Vuille, *College physics*, 8th ed. (Belmont, CA: Brooks/Cole, Cengage Learning, 2009), 119–20.

[xvii] Bährer-Kohler, 52.

[xviii] Matthew Henry, "Matthew Henry's Concise Commentary," accessed November 20, 2013,
http://biblehub.com/commentaries/mhc/exodus/20.htm.

[xix] James Luther Mays, *Amos; a Commentary* (Philadelphia, PA: Westminster Press, 1976), 144.

[xx] Borysenko, 107.

[xxi] William H. Moorcroft, *Understanding Sleep and Dreaming*, 2nd ed. (Boston, MA: Springer, 2013), 206.

[xxii] Strong, 74–75.

[xxiii] John Gill, "John Gill's Exposition of the Bible," accessed October 26, 2013, http://www.biblestudytools.com/commentaries/gills-exposition-of-the-bible/deuteronomy-5-15.html.

[xxiv] Ravi Zacharias, "Walking in Obedience Part 1," Let My People Think, accessed November 13, 2013,
http://www.oneplace.com/ministries/let-my-people-think/listen/walking-in-obedience-part-1-of-2-368910.html, starting at 9:22.

[xxv] Matthew Henry, *Matthew Henry's Commentary on the Whole Bible: Genesis to Deuteronomy-Volume 1* (New York: Hendrickson Publishers, 1992), 269.

[xxvi] "Latin definition for: vaco, vacare, vacavi, vacates," Latdict, accessed November 13, 2013, http://www.latin-dictionary.net/definition/38285/vaco-vacare-vacavi-vacatus.

[xxvii] Buttrick, Vol. 3, 727.

[xxviii] Philip Schaff and Henry Wallace, eds., *Nicene and Post-Nicene Fathers: Second Series Volume XIV: The Seven Ecumenical Councils* (New York: Cosimo Classics, 2007), 148.

[xxix] "Pulpit Commentary," accessed December 28, 2013, http://biblehub.com/commentaries/pulpit/mark/2.htm.

xxx William L. Lane, *The Gospel According to Mark*, (Grand Rapids, MI: Eerdmans, 1974), 119–20.

xxxi "Keyword Search results," Biblegateway.com, accessed November 15, 2013, http://www.biblegateway.com/keyword/?search=sabbath&version1= NIV&searchtype=all&limit=none&wholewordsonly=no&resultspp= 250&displayas=short&sort=bookorder.

xxxii R. T. France, *The Gospel According to Matthew: an Introduction and Commentary* (Leicester, England: Inter-Varsity Press, 1992), 114.

About the Author

From birth Andrew Gilmore had the privilege of being churched including several years during which his father, David, also served as his pastor. Andrew graduated from the University of Oklahoma with a degree in English. When he's not contemplating spiritual matters, he spends his time wrangling four children with his wife Katie. He writes weekly on his website at AndrewGilmore.net.

Made in the USA
Las Vegas, NV
19 June 2021